UNDER THAT SILKY ROOF

Elizabeth Robinson

UNDER THAT SILKY ROOF

Burning Deck, Providence

Acknowledgments:

The author would like to thank the editors of the following journals for publishing these poems, sometimes in earlier versions: *Five Fingers Review, Fourteen Hills, The Germ, Interim, Kenning, Lingo, New American Writing, Re: reference press, Rooms, Syllogism, Volt.*

The publication of this book was made possible by a gift in memory of Toni Warren. Burning Deck also thanks Paol Keineg, Shelby Matthews and Peter Quartermain.
Burning Deck Press is the Literature Program of ANYART: CONTEMPORARY ARTS CENTER, a tax-exempt (501c3), non-profit organization.

The cover reproduces Fran Herndon's painting "In the Wild Lagoon."

for Fran Herndon

CONTENTS

FALLING OFF THE LEDGE

—— COAST

i.

The idea of an edge is
the idea of return

Dismiss tides:
they do not come back

they are recreated

Egg and sperm fall off
the ledge
Commingling

is a loose term for the ocean

ii.

A golden egg balances
on the slat of a fence

"I want," he says
hefting it

"But someone put it here
on purpose   Leave it
there, so they'll find
it again"
"Then if not this one," he says
"we should get one like it"

iii.

The possibility of finding again
fills up all space

We swim on this abstract shore

Irreplaceability

likewise is an idea —
holding to one's breast
the singular thing

Foam, gritty water, and waves
all expand

iv.

The next day
the golden egg is still there

Fog erases the boundaries
of the coast, underlining them

Small bodies sleep in amniotic
mist, but roll slowly

absently, toward the precipice
Such arms as hypothesis

prepare to catch them

v.

Golden egg on the narrow
shelf   Maternal sunlight

licks a finger to dab
the face clean   Things

drift in and out . . .   poorly
erased   Occasionally

the egg tumbles but never breaks

From the curb, passerby

do their best to put it back
in its original place

vi.

Be reminded that
to coast is also to glide

No use in evaluating:
there's irrevocable movement

among the silver leaves
which guard that golden

substance in the nest

or pickets

MUCH ELSE BLUFF

i.

But
it's not morning

The commentary
I claim

a stolen bed
is more safe

as he falls upon me
the softness of algae

saying good-bye
upside down

ii.

One would
leave the jaw to open herself

permitting its heat to come in

its ache, back of the door

herself

interrupting itself
with ringing

These currents

belling, counter-clockwise or not

iii.

The floor
and its rising voice

being tuned

—— INTERRUPTING THE GOWN

i.

Clutterer
in rows of silver
and green

An aisle

A hedge

An order; aerial

ii.

Where the ones who recount
preside

and blend their
sparse red
and green

I hesitate to stutter

For down there

it's foam
or tiny pieces of it

Its interned softness
and
much else
bluff

Lichen, inhaling
sparse grainy nerves

iii.

Why call

that small finger
'pinky'

A land hidden between landscapes

where she squeezes out rain
from that small finger

that ends her right hand

iv.

Honey
buried in fluid

Its ora

always its
dolor

v.

But left-handed

I led furrows down the paving
Veritable

"seed of grace"

vicious seed of memory

vi.

An errant focus
makes

our philandering

breath conflict with

end

of day

or hire

Pause for you
copying the line

I foresee

vii.

By rule
to hang the window
with a mirror

Mirror backward of the door

to the recalcitrant ocean

stealing the day
to launder its clothes

viii.

Inane, both, hands after the sweet

interrupting its warping, melting

its pure, fat
infant

my mouth trained to

My clasp

fell away

such inhospitable devotion

ix.

By inability
I mean desire

Better not
to be any less respectful

on top of the house

in the stress of its white gown

x.

Interval:

blood pricked

tarries between

tasks

approaching, everything

midday

xi.

Unemployable horn
bending
night's hours

in half

Kind guardian

Fog
to any who could not arrive

Circumventing
I would say
the nest of down

trailing me

ITS CUMULUS INFANCY

—— THE RECORD

i.

You were right to proscribe movement
The record

whose third party says "sub-aqueous"

of a lost transfer

But a sort of resplendence could abide

in me as the complicated engagement
of my fingers

suggests

        that is, there is little to view as yet —

stippling, submarine those blue lines
and off-center

the signature of the aureole is slightly broadened
       and overhead its cumulus infancy

ii.

"Alright," the action comments of itself:

like a child's game, the palest green, the palest blue,
one seed by virtue of dexterity

       implanted into another

No borders may touch
to outline this twilit profile

       crowning the breath with nares,
teeth, stubble, the particular

clarity of respiration in darkness

What chews or speaks or gambols
under that silky roof

       Who calls

       the assent

iii.

An almost benign being
bit from within my right hip

which is left-handed

     Now he

carries that blue seed hardening
in his mouth

I walk from side to side
under the expansion of ribs

whose fur can also nip and fold
into circularity

     Creature, if you are, you

come back by command,
swimming in this green soup

There I submerge my own hands
apparently catching your breath

inside the immobility of my own shape-change

i.

In the loaf of bread
this core

     of undissolved milk

Container to be placed
on a sleeping woman's chest
     (It is always sleeping)

this mute, its thingness

     To fold involuntarily

or to make covenant

The quality of bread as protection

as its sleep wanders elsewhere

ii.

The leg cannot fold
into the chest

Its lassitude:
ripe fruit pressed into gut or groin

      And both concluding
the same way,
appearing able to continue

iii.

Her

corporeal reference

pointing liquidly to omission,

to what unfooted augmentation —

What promise charges this:

like an embryo, at a slant,

unavailing

iv.

Discharged its harm

The promise is to uncover the cavity,

to mispronounce, to contract

would be a portent of expansion

To watch, for example, to observe by duty

what rises, lamed and silken in its poured state

v.

Hand, hand, foot, and that correct side

undissolved in the interior

These things cannot be detached
from the globe indicated by chance

The interlocking fingers

Inside this hidden refreshment

the planet cannot demur its secret population
She would hobble there now, intersecting vows

—— GESTURE

i.

And why now,
        raking through hair and
        feathers for aerial structure,

        fingering the minimal gauge

                A bird in the hand,
                tame as an egg,
                but redundant

        Figure whose winged digits plummet

this soothing gasp:

twigs, let-down,
hope's trickery

ii.

"Sparrow"

says the son to the mother
as all such are "sparrow"

and she arrests him,
her hand, studies:

some disappointment
        alights the tree,

her nimbleness:

        Here, come —
        hold beak to blemish   Say

a long avian melody,

a loop-the-loop

choked from the posse of feathers

iii.

What pleasure to draw forth
and to break

the shell

This term would be vicarious,

this collection of down in the pillow

Knuckling, land-borne
uprising posed from a distance

i.

"Mum, mum, mum," what do you babble —
must be the quavering shadow
of smoke

"Wah," then, is water in blindness —

agile, quicker agitation

flowing uphill

alliterates into this

    clear space, a foreign language

        Buzzing here a yellowjacket
        or other

predator of flesh:
        blood's honey in the milk
        you cry for every so often

Yours,
dryness or fullness
        Contagious
or slept through

ii.

     Night in yellow
stripes,

sibilant infant

in the words beginning with "B"
lined or banded

They sting that
"only want their portion"

Beginning in the scorch-coated

red bottle-brush tree

     And a figure curved
     fetal among those red filaments

HOLLOW WHOSE
FASTENINGS DISSOLVE

—— RESERVOIR

i.

The pool
who counters gravity
digests

anew
or multiple

the pool itself, frond-like

Its fleshly theory

From the breeze falls a gesture

Pruned and fragrant aspiration

ii.

You see the blandishments

Sun on his human chest

Awkward, making way

Parts strewn along a figurative hallway

bright through

his way of distress, held fast

Glare over
swelter:
a fist stuffed in the mouth

Upward of novelty
his genuine newness

iii.

      Reflection swayed re-
      collection

           as if this, a center or hump —

How can the new one
enunciate

his nocturnal head

amid what sustains

so distinct

and what nourishes

Awaken
splayed

facing the mirror

iv.

Divided by halves:
which wee hour

revises all?

A hollow whose fastenings

dissolve

Vagrant:

in the middle of those who breathe, air wanders

v.

This late, single knowledge
clad in warmth

Suffusing the end
he drops off

The study required
in similarities

The pleasure of how

over-

due the reflection it is

vi.

Not deriding perfection
but counting on it

to backtrack
loudly

Lost, abrupted, behind

                              as to the ear:

astonishment of
waves, hummed interruption

vii.

As far as the eye can see

the legs of the breath, every animal
and human

Snoring, their moist brown leaves

Respiring
who waits outside the door

or recovering
with so patient a grasp

Comprises

Arranges some intentions

unevenly its white lung-like piece

viii.

His unintentional box-shaped, bed-like

Retrieval

is shaped as a room

Transcribed sideways, the door

in the darkness

appetite's shape

ix.

Extracting a sample
who scrawls

sees the script floating

from its kneeling position

This life

This life holds only
the heat at bay

holds purely descriptive function

x.

Truth in the form of a knob

turned in a doorless way

The summer he was made to consider
vanishes

again and over

Reflection's twin

xi.

Three steps forward,
one askew

          The cipher

untended in a large house

Message of the noon

Mug

of water
dipped from the pool   Unsteady gait

welling out
its own arrival

xii.

Reservoir
as that small body without symmetry

requited again

We hold the face

or this

very near

       Ledge:

so much
by range of sight

WITNESS

—— LARGER

The girth of the world stretches

unpretty, but

tidy

    Or its blankness

judged as good, the dark

reassurance:

as just now I hear

a human coughing from the other

side of the wall

The cough

assesses the echo as only

more itself

So expansion is refused growth, but given memory

A fetus in the esophagus

positing its loss of privacy

Some voice necessitates

that orderly gestation we don't

retract as world, the imperturbable

breath whichever direction it takes

in relation to a lung   To

end here, I hear

that irritable wall venturing

life   The breast enlarging

unsure how to lead itself

Some possible infant wandering

through the body of this

stilted respiration, some possible

fumbling of the intermediate span

— PACT

i.

Pain
stamped with a small object in flight

looks to the left when drenched and
right to be made dry

What indicates also blots out
the target   I would rather

antennae on me that
became pliable

A person to talk to,
inside me, the small tugs

folding back the blue skin
I see my bare ceiling

And around the sink
what should be heeling
but blue filaments,

their ribbon sound

can't protect me from the wet,
coming as they do to where I bathe

ii.

I would read what "you" say
but all the time feel the thread

running down my spine

I suspect what I hear,
altered as it is by my attention

The kinds, the kind: its affect

Then, where I can't raise
an adequate hand

to block out that simple glare,

the wavering antennae at the
rise, a circumspect flood

I prefer to look at what is not left
or right, but obscured by scrolling,
catching at the faded threads

To my figure I adjure patience
where the skin absolutely will not

give hard light,
digest,
glimpse the bladder

of

iii.

I practice making the shield,
the hand placed inside the belly

against that leftward light

Disconsolate, incubate,

a fraction of which does reduce

as it waxes

An ambidextrous warmth
ringed twice
in the limited cold of the season

Now arbitrary because innate:

that is, to awaken stiffly,

craning through direction

itself, its self inhabited

to the place that gapes

iv.

Penultimate only of a fold,

who
will be disappointed if
I find nothing I can repeat

A formation
as specific as it is recessed

The cleansing breath
affronts the rain   Witness:

and if the left and the right
are untrustworthy, I deplore

what above and below might mean

Two windows of four which look onto nothing,
impatient of waiting

Say the hand itself could be impregnated
Clouds, you say,

but from now on

the lack of distinction is mostly what
obtrudes on me physically

—— HAMMOCK

i.

This is how infinitely small things come to rest

They are not captive, but in relation to enclosure

who sidles out

When the mother sleeps, she has no speech,
but breathes falteringly

Alone, the bed's surface touches
a kind of skin

If the child were to have a mouth, it would be
open, and its eyes too

partially aslant

ii.

How do I dedicate

the poles of a shrinking pivot

reworded as my son

Wh-what is the blanket made of,

how do we hang there

iii.

If a woman were enough preoccupied
with shrinkage

she might have a small child

'Enough' is the sense of it

A mother stutters

The redundancy is tiredness,
could it be made drowsiness

There they are in the bed

The child is a pea under the mattress
they balance so high over

ANTHOLOGIES:
Norma Cole, ed./trans.,Crosscut Universe: Writing on Writing from France. 160 pp.
One Score More: The Second 20 Years of Burning Deck 1982-2002. Eds. Alison Bundy, K. & R. Waldrop. 240 pp.
Pegasus Descending: A Book of the Best Bad Verse (anthology). Eds. James Camp, X.J.Kennedy, and Keith Waldrop. 238 pp.

POETRY:
Beth Anderson, Overboard. 80 pp.
Rae Armantrout, Precedence. 48 pp.
Anthony Barnett, Poem About Music. 64 pp.
Mei-mei Berssenbrugge, The Heat Bird. 64 pp.
Erica Carpenter, Perspective Would Have Us. 72 pp.
Tina Darragh, Striking Resemblance. 64 pp.
Michael Davidson, The Landing of Rochambeau. 80 pp.
Patrick Fetherston, The World Was a Bubble. 52 pp.
Susan Gevirtz, Hourglass Transcripts. 70pp.
Peter Gizzi, Artificial Heart. 96 pp.
Barbara Guest, The Countess from Minneapolis. 46 pp.
Lisa Jarnot, Some Other Kind of Mission. 112 pp.
Julie Kalendek, Our Fortunes. 56 pp.
Damon Krukowski, 5000 Musical Terms. 28 pp.
Jessica Lowenthal, as if in turning. 28 pp.
Jackson Mac Low, The Virginia Woolf Poems. 44 pp.
Tom Mandel, Realism. 80 pp.
Jennifer Martenson, Xq28. 20 pp.
Harry Mathews, Out of Bounds. 28 pp.
Lissa McLaughlin, Seeing the Multitudes Delayed.76 pp.
—, Troubled by His Complexion.128 pp.
David Miller, Stromata. 64 pp.
Claire Needell, Not A Balancing Act. 64 pp.
Gale Nelson, stare decisis. 142 pp.
—, ceteris paribus. 128 pp.
Ray Ragosta, Varieties of Religious Experience. 80 pp.
Pam Rehm, The Garment In Which No One Had Slept. 64 pp.
Stephen Rodefer, Passing Duration. 64 pp.
Brian Schorn, Strabismus. 64 pp.
Keith Waldrop, Analogies of Escape. 80 pp.
—, The Space of Half an Hour. 88 pp.
Craig Watson, After Calculus. 72 pp.

Marjorie Welish, The Windows Flew Open. 80 pp.
Elizabeth Willis, Turneresque. 96 pp.
Xue Di, Heart Into Soil, trans. Keith Waldrop with Wang Ping, Iona Crook, Janet Tan and Hil Anderson. 96pp.

FICTION:
Walter Abish, 99: The New Meaning. 112 pp.
Tom Ahern, The Capture of Trieste. 66 pp.
Alison Bundy, Duncecap. 128 pp.
Robert Coover, The Grand Hotels (of Joseph Cornell). 64 pp.
Barbara Einzig, Life Moves Outside. 64 pp.
Janet Kauffman, Five on Fiction. 64 pp.
Elizabeth MacKiernan, Ancestors Maybe. 160 pp.
Jane Unrue, The House. 64 pp.
Dallas Wiebe, Going to the Mountain. 192 pp.
—, Skyblue's Essays. 160 pp.
—, The Vox Populi Street Stories. 312 pp.

SéRIE D'ECRITURE:
Anne-Marie Albiach, A Geometry (poetry), trans. K. & R. Waldrop. 26 pp.
Pierre Alferi, OXO (poetry), trans. Cole Swensen. 88 pp.
Marcel Cohen, The Peacock Emperor Moth (stories), trans. Cid Corman. 112 pp.
Jean Daive, A Lesson in Music (poem), trans. Julie Kalendek. 64 pp.
Jean Grosjean, An Earth of Time(poem), trans. Keith Waldrop . 96 pp.
Emmanuel Hocquard , A Test of Solitude (poem), trans. R. Waldrop. 72pp.
Paol Keineg, Boudica (poem), trans. Keith Waldrop. 64 pp.
Pascal Quignard, Sarx (poem), trans. Keith Waldrop. 40 pp.
—, On Wooden Tablets: Apronenia Avitia (novel), trans. Bruce X. 112 pp.
Jacqueline Risset, The Translation Begins (poetry), trans. Jennifer Moxley.96 pp.
Claude Royet-Journoud, i.e. (poem), trans. Keith Waldrop. 20 pp.
Esther Tellermann, Mental Ground (poem), trans. K. Waldrop. 80 pp.
Alain Veinstein, Even a Child (poetry), trans. R. Kocik/ R. Waldrop. 64 pp.

DICHTEN =:
Elke Erb, Mountains in Berlin (poems), trans. R. Waldrop. 96 pp.
Ludwig Harig, The Trip to Bordeaux (stories), trans. Susan Bernofsky. 104 pp.
Ernst Jandl, reft and light. A selection of poems with multiple translations by American poets. 112 pp.
Friederike Mayröcker, Heiligenanstalt (prose), trans. R. Waldrop. 96 pp.
Oskar Pastior, Many Glove Compartments (selected poems), trans. H. Mathews, C. Middleton, R. Waldrop, 120 pp.
Ilma Rakusa, Steppe (stories), trans. Solveig Emerson-Möring. 80 pp.
Gerhard Roth, The Will to Sickness (novel), trans. Tristram Wolff, 120pp.
Gerhard Rühm, i my feet: selected poems & constellations. 120 pp.

This book was designed and computer typeset   by Rosmarie Waldrop in 10 pt. Palatino. Printed on 55 lb. Writers' Natural (an acid-free paper), smyth-sewn and glued into paper covers by McNaughton & Gunn in Saline, Michigan. The cover reproduces Fran Herndon's painting, "In the Wild Lagoon." There are 1000 copies, of which 50 are numbered & signed.